2019
NEW
TESTAMENT

LESSON JOURNAL

for youth and children
By Shannon Foster

A companion journal to use along with
Come, Follow Me —
For Individuals and Families: New Testament 2019

TABLE OF CONTENTS

TIPS & IDEAS

Parents, below are some ideas and tips to help you use these journals with your children as you study the New Testament together. Read through them and take note of your favorite ideas.

Use along with your family study. As you study the New Testament this year, these journals can help your children take meaningful notes, remember what they learned, record their own inspired thoughts, and take notes of their favorite scriptures. You may want to keep these journals in a special place, along with your other New Testament teaching materials.

Adapt to your children's abilities. These journals can be used for multiple ages, from non-readers to teenagers. For non-readers, have the children draw pictures, or tell you their thoughts as you record them in their journals.

Variety is best. These journals can help make learning exciting; and as your children fill up the pages, they can reflect back on lessons they learned. Most children like new things and new approaches, so changing how they use their journals each week can make these journals especially exciting and effective. Below are some ideas with different ways the journals can be used.

> **Make a list.** Have them list the people that appear in a story, significant events in a story, or what is taught about a certain doctrine or principle.
>
> **Draw a visual.** There are many opportunities to draw something to help increase understanding. They might draw a map of Israel, draw the original twelve apostles with their names written underneath, draw a miracle that Jesus performed, make a diagram of the miracles in one chapter, draw about one of Christ's teachings, etc.
>
> **Draw a storyboard.** A storyboard is a sequence of drawings that tell a story (like a comic strip). Children could draw out a story and write what is happening under each picture.
>
> **Record a favorite phrase.** Help your children search through the scripture verses to find a favorite phrase and invite them to write it in their journals. They could even turn it into an artistic drawing.
>
> **Write your testimony about something.** From time to time you may feel the desire to write in your children's journals your personal testimony about something that was taught in a lesson. These pages could be great treasures for your children. You could also ask other family members to send you their testimonies about a topic you are studying and tape those testimonies into your children's journals.
>
> **Answer a question.** Before the lesson begins, you could write a question on their journal page that you want your children to be able to confidently answer by the end of the lesson.
>
> **Make goals.** As your children seek to apply the scriptures to their own lives, have them write their personal goals in their journals.
>
> **Keep inspired notes.** For older children, they may want to use their journals in their own way and simply write their own notes. Teaching them to write down what they are learning can help them learn to recognize personal revelation.
>
> **Write a favorite scripture (and memorize it).** Have your children pick out a favorite scripture from a chapter you are studying, write it in their journals, and memorize it.
>
> **Record testimony.** After a lesson about an important doctrine or principle, invite them to record their personal testimonies about that doctrine or principle. Invite everyone to share what they wrote (this can help the Spirit testify of truths, and strengthen their confidence in bearing testimony out loud).
>
> **Write an experience.** As you learn about principles that apply to your lives, have them write down experiences they have had regarding that principle. They could also record stories you tell them about your life or lives of their ancestors.

* We would love to see some of your journal pages or pictures of your family learning these lessons. Please tag us on Instagram @redheadedhostess, or contact us through our website.

Here is a simple diagram of the Plan of Salvation. You can start by writing what you know about each part of the Plan. Then, throughout the year as you learn about different details of the Plan, come to this page and draw pictures or write notes about what you learn.   For example, if you learn something about the Spirit World, come to this page and either in or around the circle that represents the Spirit World, write (or draw) what you learned.

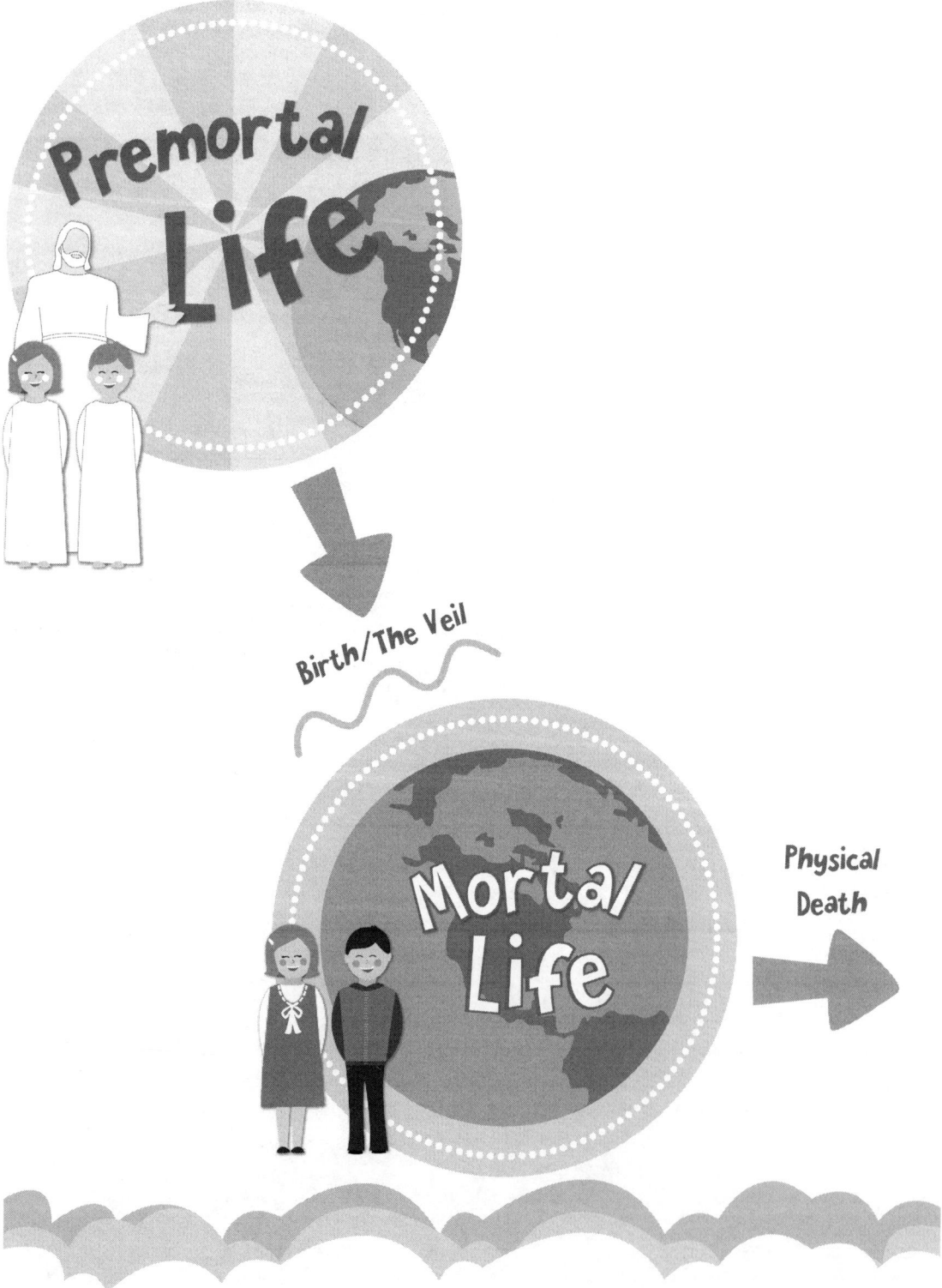

Premortal Life

Birth/The Veil

Mortal Life

Physical Death

Celestial kingdom

Resurrection

Final Judgment

Terrestrial kingdom

Spirit World

Telestial kingdom

We Are Responsible
FOR OUR OWN LEARNING

How can we make our home more
GOSPEL CENTERED?

What is a
FAMILY COUNCIL?

A family council is a meeting on any day of the week. It can be with just you and a parent or with your whole family. It's a time when you can …

Turn off electronics and look at and listen to each other.

Tell your parents about your worries or fears.

Offer to help a sibling during a hard time.

Make goals and write them down.

Combined with prayer, a family council can invite the Savior's presence in your home. It can help your family be happy.

(The Friend, July 2017)

5

Matthew 1; Luke 1
BE IT UNTO ME ACCORDING TO THY WORD

WHO WAS MATTHEW?

Matthew was one of the Twelve Apostles.

Matthew was an eyewitness to many things he wrote about.

Before he was an apostle, Matthew was a publican, which was a tax collector.

Matthew was writing to Jews. His purpose was to show that Jesus Christ fulfilled the messianic prophecies of the Old Testament.

_____
_____
_____
_____
_____
_____
_____
_____
_____
_____
_____
_____
_____
_____
_____
_____
_____

WHO WAS LUKE?

Luke wrote this book as well as the Book of Acts.

Many scholars believe that Luke was a physician.

Luke wrote to the Gentiles. He wrote about the Savior's mission and ministry so that those who read could "know the certainty" (Luke 1:4) of the Savior.

Luke was not an eyewitness of the Savior. He gained his understanding and testimony from others who were "eyewitnesses and ministers of the Word".

Luke 2; Matthew 2
WE HAVE COME TO WORSHIP HIM

DID YOU KNOW?

Did you know that the scriptures never say that there were three Wise Men? The scriptures tell us that Wise Men from the East came to worship Jesus and brought three gifts (gold, frankincense, and myrrh). Many assume that each Wise Man brought a gift, so they think that there were three Wise Men. But it could have been two, three, four, or more that brought those three gifts.

WHY DO YOU THINK
THE ANGELS SENT SHEPHERDS
TO BE WITNESSES OF THE
BIRTH OF CHRIST?

John 1
WE HAVE FOUND THE MESSIAH

\\\|///
WHO
IS THE MESSIAH?

"Messiah" is a title that means "the anointed one" or the person chosen to be the King and the Deliverer. Jesus was the Messiah.

The Jews were waiting for the Messiah, but only some recognized Him when he came.

Messiah is an Aramaic word (the language Jesus spoke). The title "Christ" is the Greek equivalent of "Messiah."

Therefore, Jesus' last name was not Christ. He was Jesus the Christ, or Jesus the Messiah.

_____

_____

_____

_____

_____

_____

_____

_____

_____

_____

_____

_____

_____

_____

_____

_____

_____

_____

WHO WAS JOHN?

John and his brother James were fishermen at the Sea of Galilee and worked with their father, Zebedee, and Simon Peter.

John was an eyewitness to the events he recorded.

John was in the First Presidency with Peter and James.

John's account is for everyone to read but is especially for the faithful Christians.

Matthew 3; Mark 1; Luke 3
PREPARE YE THE WAY OF THE LORD

WHO WAS MARK?

Mark lived in Jerusalem.

Mark was an assistant to Peter and wrote this book based on what he learned from Peter.

Mark was writing to the Gentiles and to Christian converts.

Mark was with Paul on some of Paul's missionary journeys.

USING YOUR FOOTNOTES

On each page in your scriptures you can find footnotes printed at the bottom. The footnotes are to help you better understand something in a verse.

Let's practice using some footnotes!

Open your scriptures to Matthew 3:15. This is when Jesus was telling John the Baptist to baptize Him. In verse 14, John expressed that he did not feel like he should baptize Christ. In verse 15, Christ responded, "suffer it to be so now." Look at the footnotes in verse 15 and write what suffer means in the box below.

Matthew 4; Luke 4-5
THE SPIRIT OF THE LORD IS UPON ME

WHO IS THE DEVIL?

Satan, also called the adversary or the devil, is the enemy of righteousness and those who seek to follow God.

He is a spirit son of God who was once an angel "in authority in the presence of God" (D&C 76:25).

Satan persuaded "a third part of the hosts of heaven" to turn away from the Father (D&C 29:36).

As a result of this rebellion, Satan and his followers were cut off from God's presence and denied the blessing of receiving a physical body (see Revelation 12:9).

Heavenly Father allows Satan and Satan's followers to tempt us as part of our experience in mortality (see 2 Nephi 2:11–14; D&C 29:39).

Because Satan "seeketh that all men might be miserable like unto himself" (2 Nephi 2:27), he and his followers try to lead us away from righteousness.

You do not have to give in to Satan's temptations. You have the power within you to choose good over evil, and you can always seek the Lord's help through prayer.

Information above from
True to the Faith, "Satan"

WHAT IS ONE IMPORTANT
LESSON YOU LEARNED
IN THESE SCRIPTURES?

John 2-4
YE MUST BE BORN AGAIN

WHO ARE THE SAMARITANS?

– Open your scriptures to the Bible Maps. Find the map for the Holy Land in New Testament Times. Locate Jerusalem and find Nazareth (where Christ grew up). Now find Samaria.

– The Samaritans were part Jew and part Gentile. The Samaritans had become bitter enemies to the Jews and had built their own temple.

Matthew 5; Luke 6
BLESSED ARE YE

_____

_____

_____

_____

_____

_____

_____

_____

_____

_____

_____

_____

_____

In Matthew 5-7, Jesus gave a sermon that is often called "The Sermon on the Mount." Do you have some Bible photographs in the back of your scriptures? If you look at study help #23 ("Sea of Galilee and the Mount of Beatitudes") you will be able to see what this mount looked like. Fill the mount below with teachings from this sermon. You can write or draw them.

THE SERMON ON THE MOUNT

WHAT ARE THE BEATITUDES?

When Jesus gave His Sermon on the Mount, He began by giving eight beatitudes (Matthew 5:3-10). These are eight Christlike characteristics that we should try to develop in ourselves. List those characteristics below.

1 -

2 -

3 -

4 -

5 -

6 -

7 -

8 -

Matthew 6-7
HE TAUGHT THEM AS ONE HAVING AUTHORITY

PRAYER
What do you learn about prayer in
Matthew 6:5-8?

_____
_____
_____
_____
_____
_____
_____
_____
_____
_____
_____
_____

THE WISE MAN & THE FOOLISH MAN

Draw or write about the parable in Matthew 7:24–27.

Matthew 8-9; Mark 2-5
THY FAITH HATH MADE THEE WHOLE

WHAT IS A MIRACLE?

"A miracle is **an extraordinary event caused by the power of God**."
(*Guide to the Scriptures*, 165)

WHY DO YOU THINK THE SAVIOR PERFORMED SO MANY MIRACLES?

Matthew 10-12; Mark 2; Luke 7; 11
THESE TWELVE JESUS SENT FORTH

QUORUM of the TWELVE APOSTLES

Can you list the 12 men that Christ chose as His Twelve Apostles?
You can find their names in Matthew 10:1-4.

1. _____
2. _____
3. _____
4. _____
5. _____
6. _____

7. _____
8. _____
9. _____
10. _____
11. _____
12. _____

QUORUM of the TWELVE APOSTLES

Can you list the current 12 men that Christ has chosen to be the
Quorum of the Twelve Apostles today?

1. _____
2. _____
3. _____
4. _____
5. _____
6. _____

7. _____
8. _____
9. _____
10. _____
11. _____
12. _____

Matthew 13; Luke 8; 13
WHO HATH EARS TO HEAR, LET HIM HEAR

WHAT IS A PARABLE?

"[A parable is] a simple story used to illustrate and teach a spiritual truth or principle. A parable is based on comparing an ordinary object or event to a truth."

(Guide to the Scriptures, "Parable")

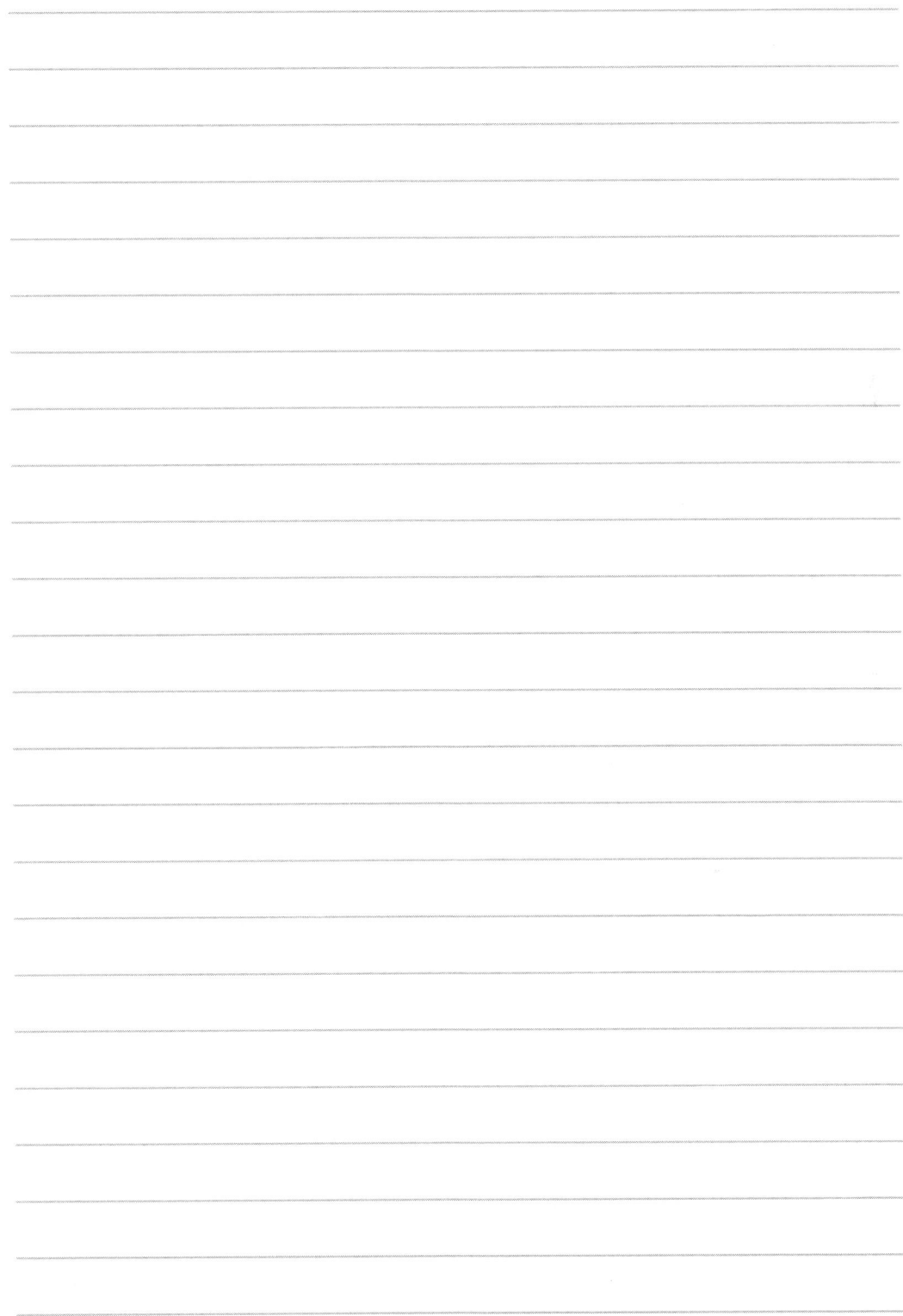

Matthew 14-15; Mark 6-7; John 5-6
"BE NOT AFRAID"

What is your favorite scripture or phrase from these chapters? Write it in this frame.

_____

_____

_____

_____

_____

_____

_____

_____

_____

_____

_____

_____

_____

What do you think it means that Jesus is the

BREAD OF LIFE?

(John 6:48–51)

Matthew 16–17; Mark 9; Luke 9
'THOU ART THE CHRIST'

How is revelation like a rock?

MATTHEW 16:18-20

Easter
"O GRAVE, WHERE IS THY VICTORY?"

_____
_____
_____
_____
_____
_____
_____
_____
_____
_____
_____
_____
_____
_____
_____
_____

What is RESURRECTION?

Resurrection is the reuniting of the spirit with the body in an immortal state, no longer subject to disease or death.

The Savior was the first person on this earth to be resurrected.

Through the Atonement of Jesus Christ, all people will be resurrected and saved from physical death.

What are your favorite things about Easter?

Matthew 18; Luke 10
"WHAT SHALL I DO TO INHERIT ETERNAL LIFE?"

_____

_____

_____

_____

_____

_____

_____

_____

_____

_____

_____

_____

_____

What did the Savior tell us to "go and do"
in Luke 10:25-37?

GO
AND
DO
THOU
LIKEWISE

John 7-10
"I AM THE GOOD SHEPHERD"

What do you think it means in John 8:12 when it says that Jesus is the "Light of the World?"

What do you think it means in John 10:1–18 and 27–29 when it says that Jesus is the "Good Shepherd?"

Luke 12-17; John 11

"REJOICE WITH ME; FOR I HAVE FOUND MY SHEEP WHICH WAS LOST"

_____

_____

_____

_____

_____

_____

_____

_____

_____

_____

_____

_____

_____

_____

_____

_____

_____

_____

_____

_____

_____

_____

_____

WHAT DOES **PRODIGAL** MEAN?

– In Luke 15:11–32 you learn about a parable called _The Parable of the Prodigal Son._ Prodigal means spending money or resources freely and recklessly; wastefully extravagant.

Matthew 19-20; Mark 10; Luke 18
'WHAT LACK I YET?'

What is ETERNAL LIFE?

Eternal life is the phrase used in scripture to define the quality of life that our Eternal Father lives.

Eternal life, or exaltation, is to live in God's presence and to continue as families (see D&C 131:1–4).

This gift is made possible through the Atonement of Jesus Christ.

To inherit eternal life requires our "obedience to the laws and ordinances of the Gospel."

Gospel Topics, "Eternal Life"

Matthew 21-23; Mark 11; Luke 19-20; John 12

'BEHOLD, THY KING COMETH'

THE LAST WEEK

These chapters teach you about the last week of Christ's life. Make a list of things that happened during this special week.

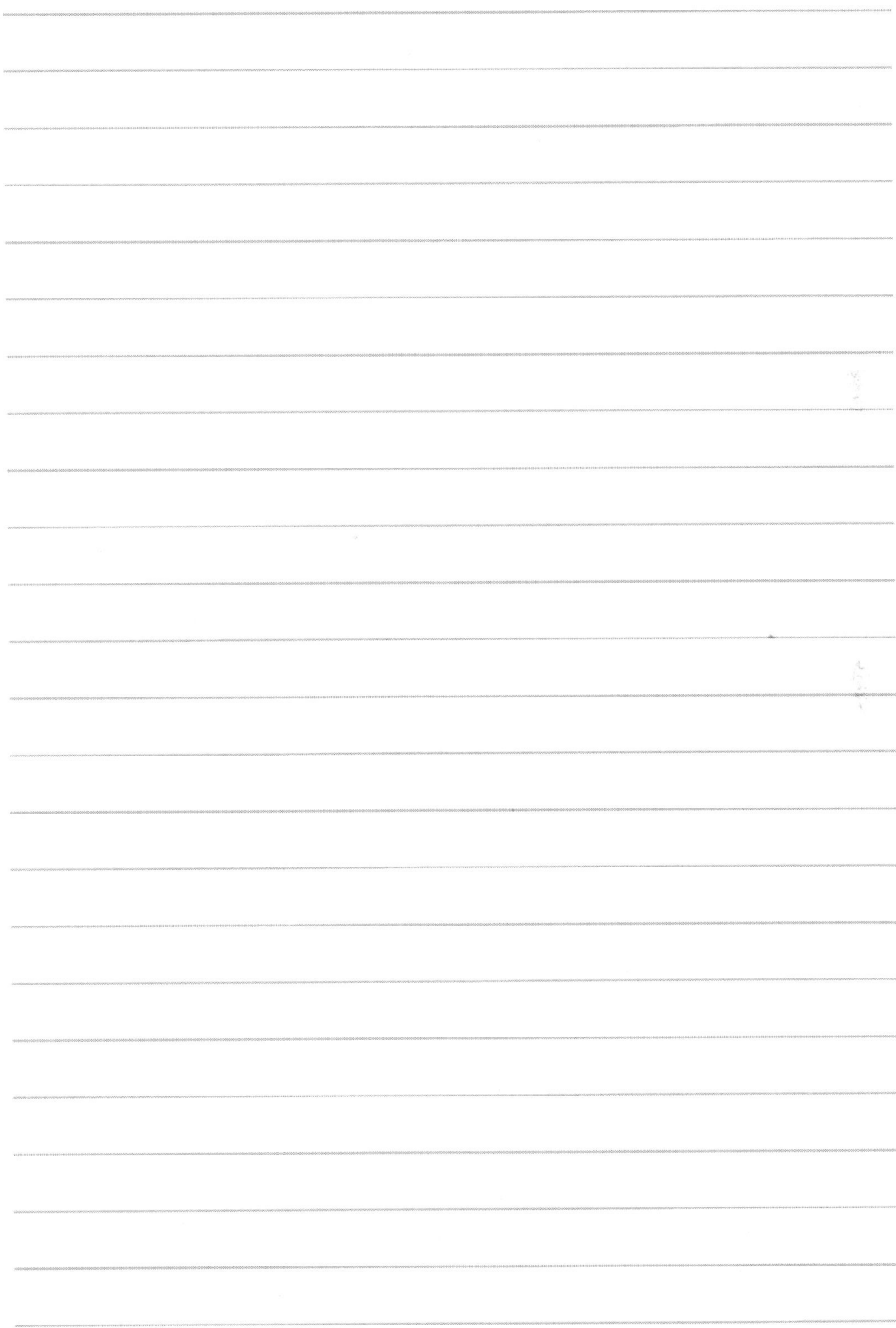

Joseph Smith—Matthew 1; Matthew 25; Mark 12-13; Luke 21
"THE SON OF MAN SHALL COME"

FILL UP
YOUR LAMP

What can you do this week to fill your spiritual lamps? How can you strengthen your testimony and be prepared for the Second Coming? Below, keep a list of things you do this week.

John 13-17
"CONTINUE YE IN MY LOVE"

_____
_____
_____
_____
_____
_____
_____
_____
_____
_____
_____
_____
_____
_____
_____
_____

DRAW A PICTURE of what Jesus wants you to do if you love Him. You can find the answer in John 14:15.

_____

_____

_____

_____

_____

_____

_____

_____

_____

_____

_____

_____

_____

_____

_____

_____

John 16:33

How has Christ overcome the world? How has His
Atonement brought your family peace and cheer?

Matthew 26; Mark 14; Luke 22; John 18
"NOT AS I WILL, BUT AS THOU WILT"

Luke 22:19-20

What do you think it would have been like to be there during the first sacrament?

What can you do to make partaking of the sacrament each week meaningful?

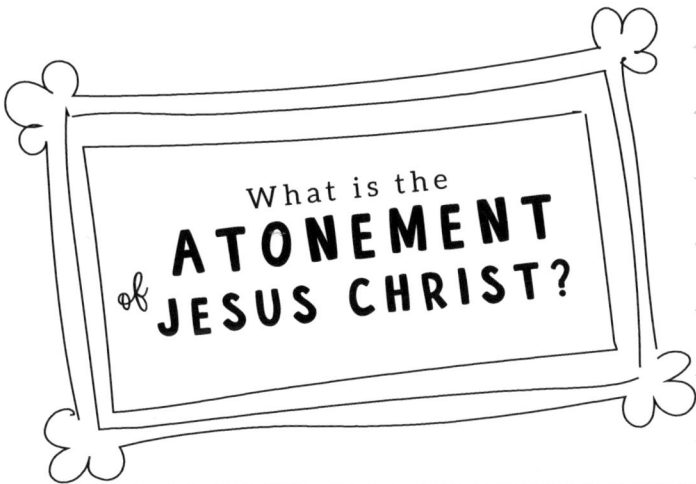

What is the ATONEMENT of JESUS CHRIST?

Heavenly Father knew that if we sinned and made mistakes, we would not be able to live with Him again. So His Son, Jesus Christ, offered to be our Savior. Heavenly Father chose Him to save us because He was the only one who could live a life without sin.

Jesus suffered and died to save us from death and our sins. This loving act is called the Atonement. Because of the Atonement, we can repent of our sins, be forgiven, and become clean and pure, as Jesus is.

The Friend, April 2011

Matthew 27; Mark 15; Luke 23; John 19
"IT IS FINISHED"

WHO WAS
PILATE?

At this time, Israel was under the power of Rome, so Rome had placed governors (or prefects) to enforce their will upon the people. Pilate was the current governor.

The Sanhedrin (the supreme Jewish council) had no power to carry out the sentence to have Christ put to death, so they needed Pilate to give that sentence.

Jesus was charged with sedition (stirring up the people against their authority) by declaring Himself a king. Pilate did not find any evidence to support the charge, but the Jewish leaders threatened to report Pilate to the Emporer of Rome, so Pilate carried out the sentence. That sentence required death.

✝ "BEHOLD THE GREAT REDEEMER DIE"

Hymn #191

In this box, record your favorite phrases from this hymn.

Matthew 28; Mark 16; Luke 24; John 20-21
"HE IS RISEN"

_____

_____

_____

_____

_____

_____

_____

_____

_____

_____

_____

_____

_____

_____

_____

WHO WERE SOME
WITNESSES
OF THE RESURRECTION?

Acts 1–5

"YE SHALL BE WITNESSES UNTO ME"

THE HOUR OF
PRAYER

In Acts 3:1, Peter and John went to the temple at the hour of prayer, which was the ninth hour. The ninth hour would have been around 3:00 P.M. The Jewish day was divided into twelve equal parts. The ninth hour would be about 3:00 P.M. This was the hour of evening prayer. Morning prayer was offered at 9:00 A.M.

IN WHAT WAYS WOULD YOU LIKE TO BE LIKE PETER AND JOHN IN ACTS 3-5?

Acts 6–9

˙WHAT WILT THOU HAVE ME TO DO?˙

STEPHEN
Acts 6:8 - 7:60

What messages did Stephen give to the Sanhedrin (the supreme Jewish council, who wanted Christ to be put to death)?

Acts 10–15
"THE WORD OF GOD GREW AND MULTIPLIED"

PETER IN PRISON
Acts 12:5

When Peter was cast into prison, the members of the Church gathered and prayed for him. Who is someone you and your family could pray for?

Acts 16-21
"THE LORD HAD CALLED US FOR TO PREACH THE GOSPEL"

WHO WAS PAUL?

Saul was born in the Greek city Tarsus and was a Roman citizen.

He was a Jew from the lineage of Benjamin and was a student of the Pharisee Gamaliel who was a respected teacher.

Saul persecuted Christians until the Lord appeared to him which changed Saul's life. After this, he will be known as Paul.

Paul was a devout missionary and traveled to many Gentile nations to preach the gospel.

Paul wrote 14 epistles which are found in your New Testament.

Paul had an eventful life including three missionary journeys, visions of the Lord, two years in prison, and a shipwreck.

Acts 18:24

What do you think it means to be "mighty in the scriptures?"

What can you do to become "mighty in the scriptures?"

Acts 22-28
"A MINISTER AND A WITNESS"

LESSONS LEARNED FROM PAUL

What are some lessons you learned from Paul in these chapters?

Romans 1-6
'THE POWER OF GOD UNTO SALVATION'

WHO WAS PAUL WRITING TO IN
ROMANS?

Paul wrote the Epistle to the Romans to members of the Church in Rome (Romans 1:7). How the Church began in Rome is not known, but is likely when Jews visiting from Rome heard Peter preach (see Acts 2:10). Though Paul had not yet been to Rome, he wrote to specific Saints he knew either by prior acquaintance or through others who had lived in Rome.

What can you do to show that you are not ashamed of the gospel of Jesus Christ?

Romans 7-16
"OVERCOME EVIL WITH GOOD"

_____

_____

_____

_____

_____

_____

_____

_____

_____

_____

YOUR HEAVENLY FATHER LOVES YOU

Romans 8:35-39

What is your testimony of your Heavenly Father's love for you?

1 Corinthians 1-7
"BE PERFECTLY JOINED TOGETHER"

_____
_____
_____
_____
_____
_____
_____
_____
_____
_____
_____
_____
_____
_____
_____
_____
_____
_____
_____
_____
_____

WHO WAS PAUL WRITING TO IN
CORINTH?

Paul wrote to Church members in the city of Corinth. Paul had preached the gospel there for nearly two years (see Acts 18:1–18). During his service there he organized a branch of the Church. While no longer in Corinth, Paul received another report from Church members in Corinth detailing problems in the Church there (see 1 Corinthians 1:11), which he responded to by writing an epistle, which became known as 1 Corinthians.

YOUR BODY IS A TEMPLE

1 Corinthians
6:19-20

What can you do to treat your
body like a temple?

1 Corinthians 8-13
'YE ARE THE BODY OF CHRIST'

WHAT ARE SOME OF YOUR
SPIRITUAL
GIFTS?
1 Corinthians 12:4-11

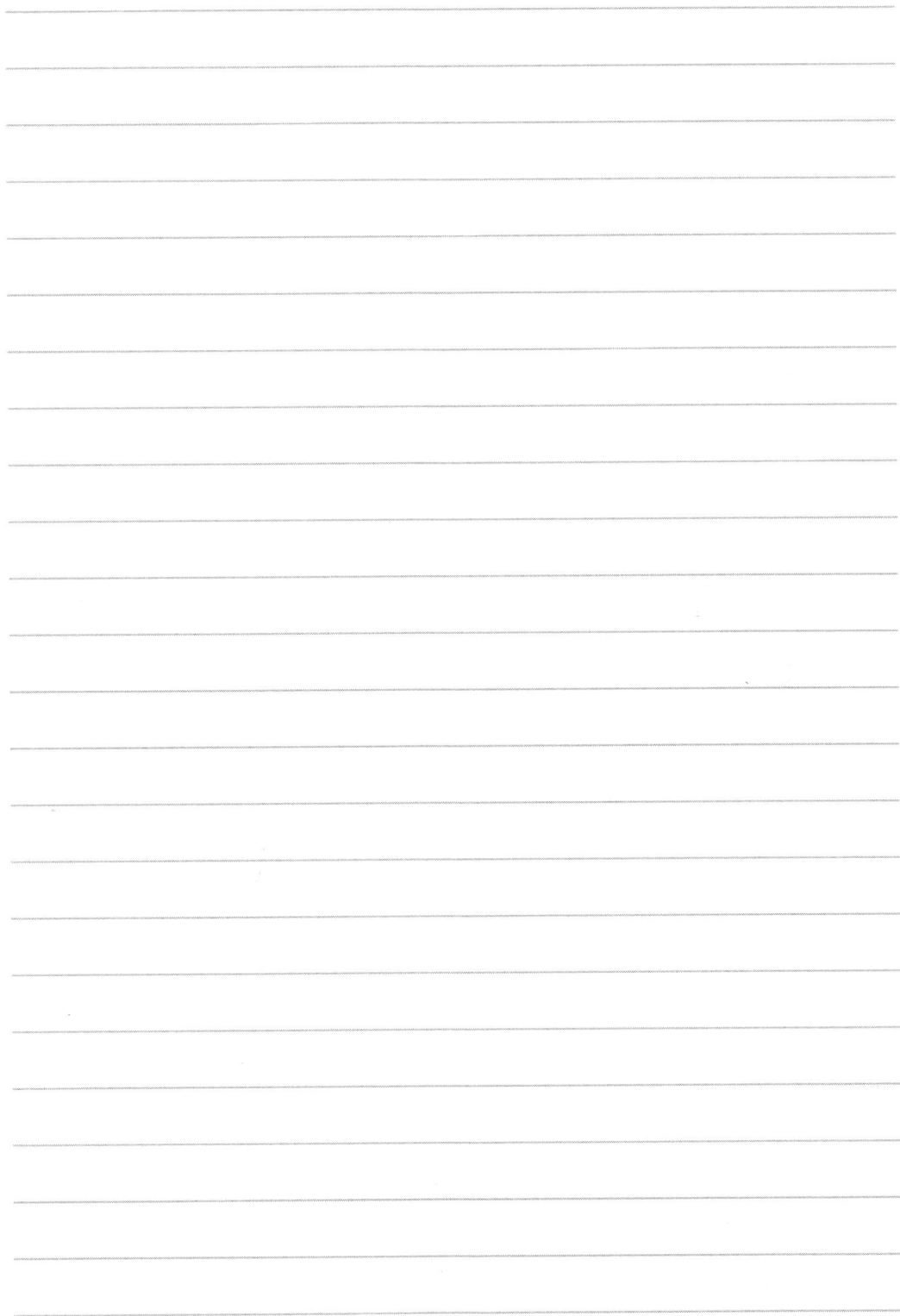

1 Corinthians 14–16

"GOD IS NOT THE AUTHOR OF CONFUSION, BUT OF PEACE"

WHAT ARE SOME TEACHINGS IN THESE CHAPTERS THAT BRING YOU COMFORT and HAPPINESS?

2 Corinthians 1-7
"BE YE RECONCILED TO GOD"

HOW CAN TRIALS BE BLESSINGS?

2 Corinthians 1:3-7

2 Corinthians 8-13
"GOD LOVETH A CHEERFUL GIVER"

A CHEERFUL GIVER
2 Corinthians 9:6-7

Who are some cheerful givers that you know?
How can you be a cheerful giver like the saints in 2 Corinthians?

Galatians
"WALK IN THE SPIRIT"

_____
_____
_____
_____
_____
_____
_____
_____
_____
_____
_____
_____
_____
_____
_____
_____
_____

WHO WAS PAUL WRITING TO IN
GALATIANS?

Paul wrote to Christians in Galatia because he was worried that they were straying from the Lord by following the teachings of some who wanted to "pervert the gospel" (see Galatians 1:6–7). Some were turning back to the Law of Moses and Paul wrote to try to persuade them to turn fully to the gospel of Jesus Christ.

FRUITS
of the
SPIRIT?

Galatians 5:22-23

Write the fruits of the Spirit
over the nine fruits.

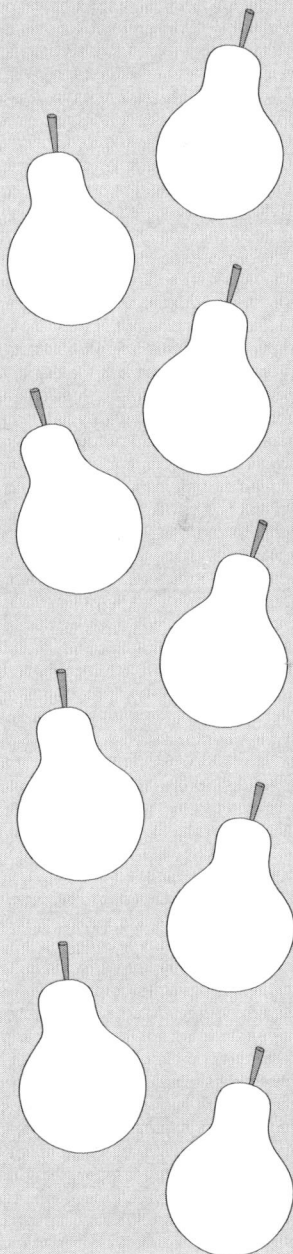

Ephesians
'FOR THE PERFECTING OF THE SAINTS'

_____

_____

_____

_____

_____

_____

_____

_____

_____

_____

_____

_____

_____

_____

_____

_____

_____

_____

_____

_____

WHO WAS PAUL WRITING TO IN
EPHESIANS?

Many scholars believe that Paul wrote this epistle to several congregations of saints, including those in Ephesus. During his third missionary journey, Paul's headquarters were in Ephesus and he loved the people there deeply.

THE ARMOUR of GOD

EPHESIANS 6:10-18

1. Color the face of the person below to look like you.
2. Study Ephesians 6:10-18 and draw the proper spiritual armour on yourself.
3. Label your armour with what it represents spiritually.

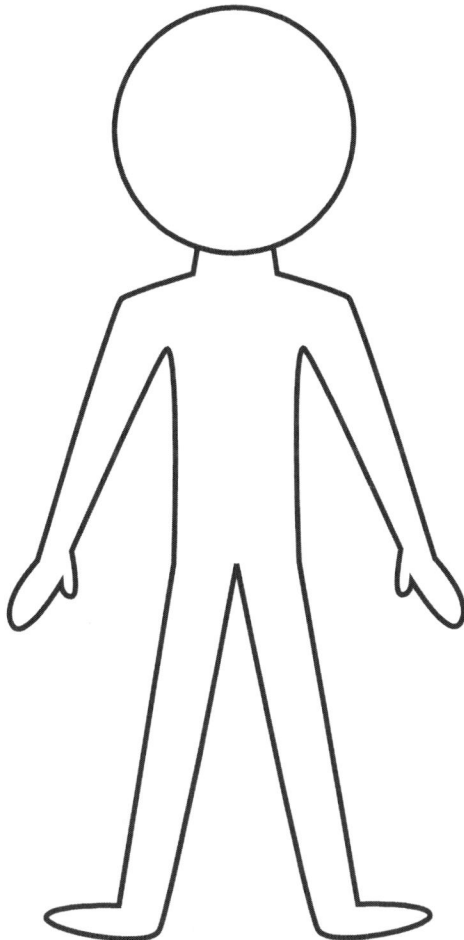

Philippians; Colossians
"I CAN DO ALL THINGS THROUGH CHRIST WHICH STRENGTHENETH ME"

How has Christ **STRENGTHENED** you *and* members of your family?

PHILIPPIANS 4:13

_____

_____

_____

_____

_____

_____

_____

_____

_____

_____

_____

_____

_____

_____

_____

_____

_____

_____

WHO WAS PAUL WRITING TO IN
PHILIPPIANS & COLOSSIANS?

Paul's first missionary journey was in Philippi and Paul established a branch of the Church there. Paul wrote to tell them thank you for what they did for him, including giving some financial help.

Paul wrote the letter to the members of the Church in Colosse, a site in modern-day Turkey. At the time he wrote this letter Paul was in prison in Rome and had heard that the Colossian saints were falling into sin.

1 and 2 Thessalonians
"BE NOT SOON SHAKEN IN MIND, OR BE TROUBLED"

WHAT IS THE
SECOND COMING
of JESUS CHRIST?

Jesus came to the earth as a newborn baby. That was His "first coming." He will come to the earth again, and we call this His "second coming."

When Jesus comes to the earth again, He will come in power and glory to claim the earth as His kingdom.

His Second Coming will be the beginning of the Millennium.

The Second Coming will be a fearful, mournful time for the wicked, but it will be a day of peace for the righteous.

The Lord has not revealed exactly when He will come again: "The hour and the day no man knoweth, neither the angels in heaven, nor shall they know until he comes" (D&C 49:7). But He has revealed to His prophets the events and signs that will precede His Second Coming.

PAUL WROTE THESE EPISTLES TO THE SAINTS IN THESSALONICA. THEY HAD MANY QUESTIONS ABOUT THE SECOND COMING OF JESUS CHRIST.

_____

_____

_____

_____

_____

_____

_____

_____

_____

_____

_____

_____

WHAT CAN YOU AND YOUR FAMILY DO TO

⟫⟫⟶ PREPARE ⟵⟪⟪

FOR THE SECOND COMING

OF JESUS CHRIST?

1 THESSALONIANS 5:1-6

1 and 2 Timothy; Titus; Philemon
"BE THOU AN EXAMPLE OF THE BELIEVERS"

_____
_____
_____
_____
_____
_____
_____
_____
_____
_____
_____
_____

WHO WAS PAUL WRITING TO IN

1 & 2 TIMOTHY, TITUS, & PHILEMON?

1 & 2 TIMOTHY: Paul served with Timothy on his second missionary journey. At the time of the epistles Timothy was serving as a Church leader in Ephesus. Paul gives Timothy counsel and guidance.

TITUS: Titus was a Greek whom Paul had baptized. Following his conversion, Titus served with Paul to preach the Gospel. Paul wrote to Titus to strengthen him as he led the Church in Crete.

PHILEMON: "This epistle is a private letter about Onesimus, a slave who had robbed his master, Philemon, and run away to Rome" (Bible Dictionary, "Pauline Epistles").

HOW CAN YOU BE AN
EXAMPLE OF
the BELIEVERS?

1 Timothy 4:12

Hebrews 1–6
JESUS CHRIST, "THE AUTHOR OF ETERNAL SALVATION"

WHO WAS PAUL WRITING TO IN
HEBREWS?

Paul wrote this letter to Hebrew Christians to help strengthen their faith in Jesus Christ and not return to their life before.

What did you learn about Jesus Christ in these chapters?

Hebrews 7-13
"AN HIGH PRIEST OF GOOD THINGS TO COME"

What do you learn about faith as you study Hebrews 11? Draw or doodle what you learn below (all around the word "faith").

FAITH

James

"BE YE DOERS OF THE WORD, AND NOT HEARERS ONLY"

JAMES 1:5-6

Why is James 1: 5–6 such an important scripture?

WHO WAS JAMES WRITING TO?

James wrote his letter "to the twelve tribes which are scattered abroad" (James 1:1), meaning all the house of Israel; he was inviting them to "receive the gospel ... [and] come into the fold of Christ" (Bruce R. McConkie, Doctrinal New Testament Commentary, 3 vols. [1965–73], 3:243).

1 and 2 Peter
"REJOICE WITH JOY UNSPEAKABLE AND FULL OF GLORY"

THE SPIRIT WORLD

What do you learn about the spirit world in 1 Peter 3:18–20 and 4:6?

_____

_____

_____

_____

_____

_____

_____

_____

_____

_____

_____

_____

_____

_____

_____

_____

_____

_____

WHO WAS PETER WRITING TO?

Peter wrote his epistle to the Roman saints with the intention of strengthening their faith.

1-3 John; Jude
'GOD IS LOVE'

[blank lined writing space]

WHO WAS JOHN WRITING TO?

It is unclear exactly who John the Beloved was writing to, other than believers or fellow saints. False teachers had been leading saints into apostasy and he writes to correct the teachings being spread abroad.

WHO WAS JUDE WRITING TO?

Jude is likely the half-brother of Jesus Christ. Jude is writing to the saints and encouraging them to stand up to the false teachers and their lies.

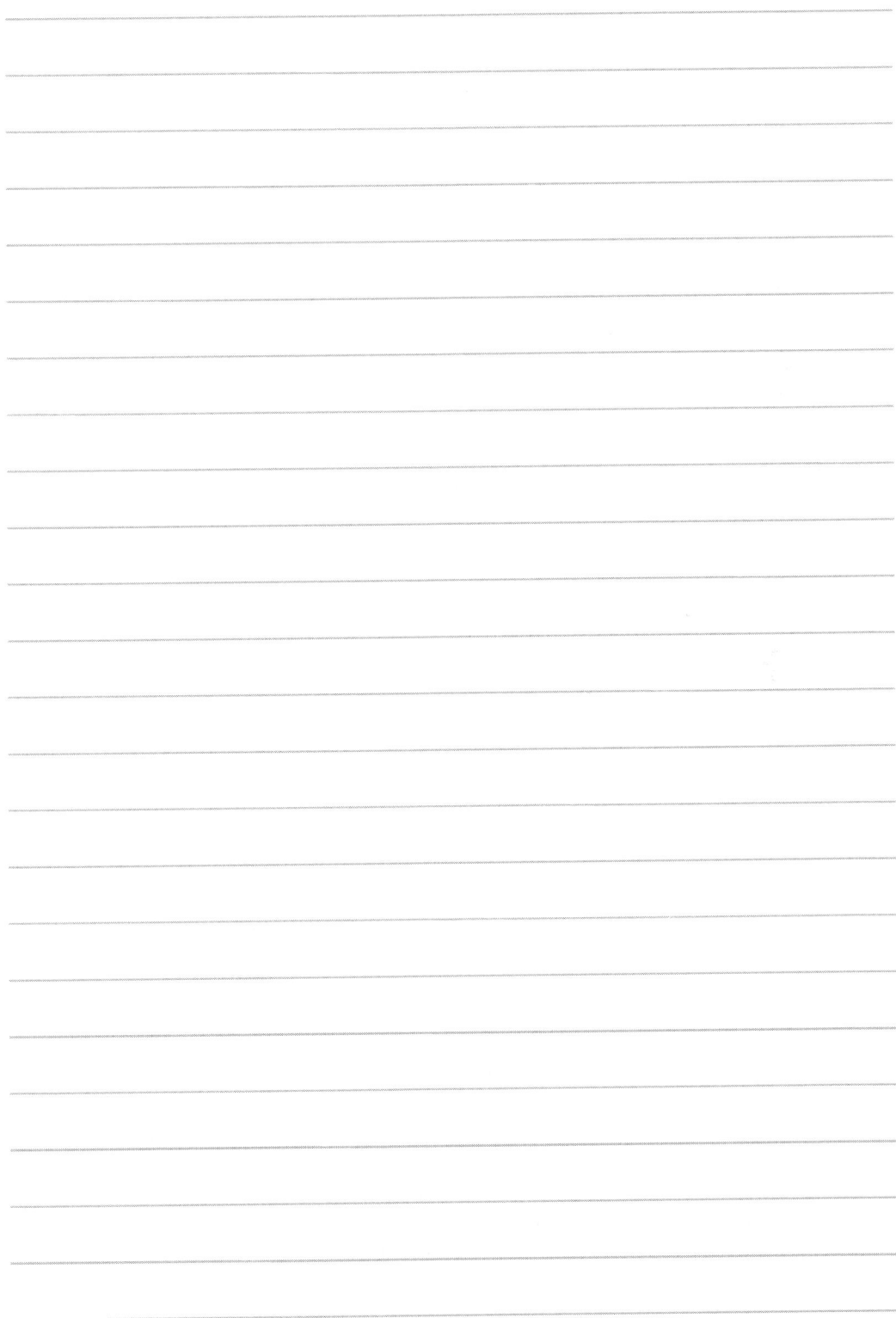

Revelation 1-11
"GLORY, AND POWER, BE UNTO ... THE LAMB FOR EVER"

_____
_____
_____
_____
_____
_____
_____
_____
_____
_____
_____
_____
_____
_____
_____
_____
_____
_____

WHAT IS THE BOOK OF REVELATION?

John the Beloved recorded a vision that he was foreordained to record (see 1 Nephi 14:18-27). In this vision, John reveals Jesus Christ's central role in Heavenly Father's Plan of Salvation. He also gives a history of the world including events and circumstances of the Last Days, the Second Coming, and the Millennium.

What did you learn about Jesus
Christ in these chapters?

Christmas

"GOOD TIDINGS OF GREAT JOY"

WHAT ARE YOUR FAVORITE THINGS ABOUT CHRISTMAS?

FAVORITE THINGS

Revelation 12-22

"HE THAT OVERCOMETH SHALL INHERIT ALL THINGS"

WHAT DO THESE CHAPTERS TEACH YOU
ABOUT THE IMPORTANCE OF YOU AND YOUR FAMILY
PREPARING
FOR THE SECOND COMING
OF JESUS CHRIST?

WHAT ARE YOUR
FAVORITE STORIES
IN THE NEW TESTAMENT?

WHAT HAVE YOU LEARNED ABOUT
JESUS CHRIST
AS YOU HAVE STUDIED THE NEW TESTAMENT?

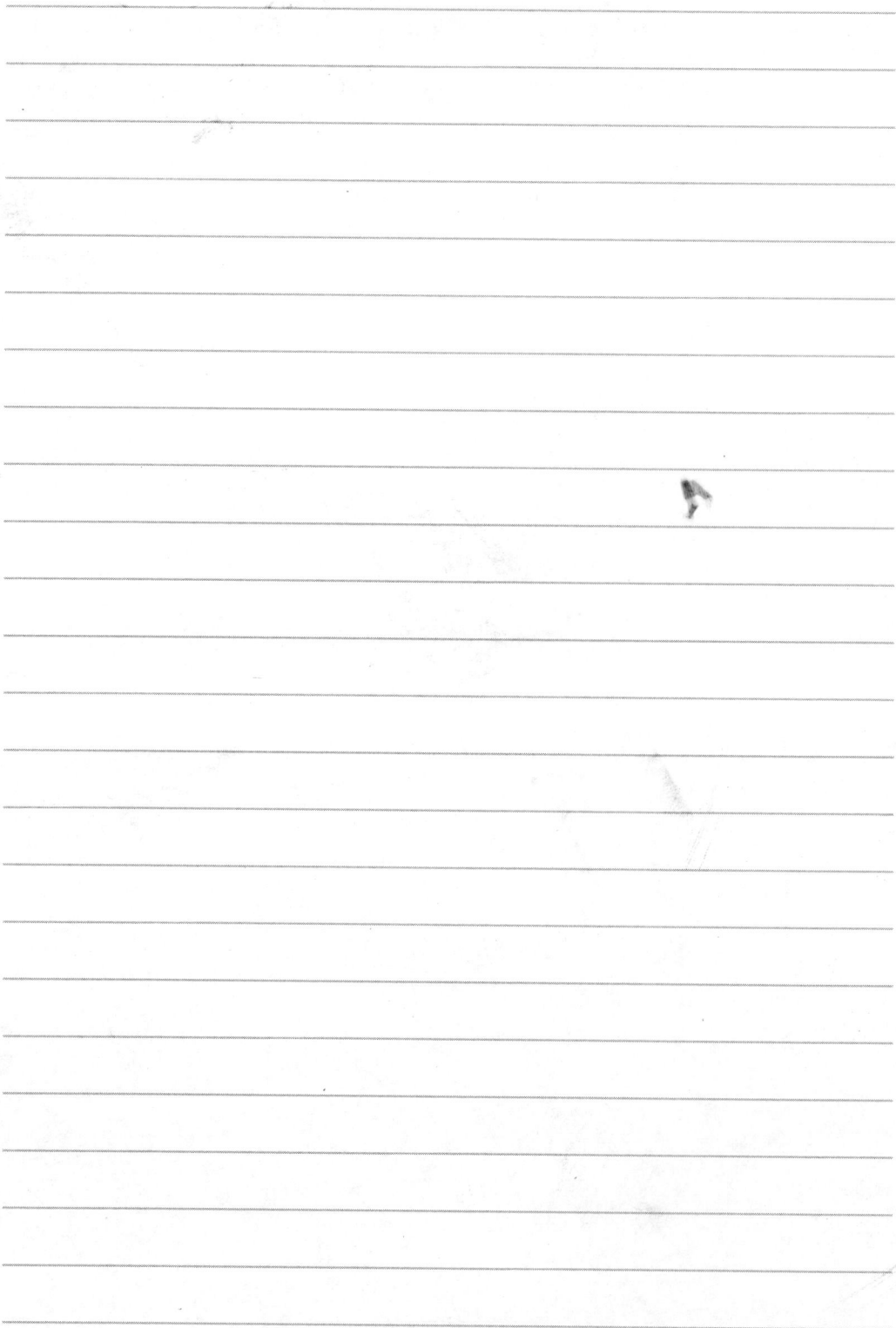